The Art of Mandala²

Adult Coloring Books
By
Jason Hamilton

Copyright © 2019 Adult Coloring Books By Jason Hamilton, LLC
All rights reserved.

No part of this book may be reproduced, transmitted, or stored in any form or by any means except for your own personal use or for a book review, without the express written permission of the author:

jason@jasonhamilton.ink

ISBN 978-1-944845-13-1

Thank you for purchasing my coloring book!

I am an independent artist, and all artwork you see in my coloring books are hand drawn by my own hand. I hope you're happy with my artwork and it has exceeded your expectations. If you have time, please share your experience with other shoppers on Amazon by leaving my book a review.

This coloring book is printed and distributed exclusively on Amazon. In the rare case that you find any print defects, Amazon has an amazing return policy, you can always exchange the book for a new copy.

If you have any questions, please don't hesitate to send me an email:

jason@jasonhamilton.ink

For more information, including tutorials, free downloads, and my coloring groups, please visit:

www.jasonhamilton.ink

Color Swatch

Test your color supplies on this page to see how they react to the paper. Place a blank page or two behind each page as you color, to prevent bleed-through to the next page.

If you enjoyed this coloring book, you might also be interested in the original:

The Art of Mandala, Volume 1
Available on Amazon.com

Don't forget to check out my other books, join my mailing list, and download free prints at

www.JasonHamilton.ink

Made in the USA
Coppell, TX
10 November 2020